**FOCUS ON
FAMILY
MATTERS**

Dealing with
Terminal Illness
in the Family

FOCUS ON FAMILY MATTERS

Focus on Family Matters

Dealing with Terminal Illness in the Family

Heather Lehr Wagner

Marvin Rosen, Ph.D.
Consulting Editor

Chelsea House Publishers
Philadelphia

CHELSEA HOUSE PUBLISHERS

EDITOR IN CHIEF Sally Cheney
DIRECTOR OF PRODUCTION Kim Shinners
CREATIVE MANAGER Takeshi Takahashi
MANUFACTURING MANAGER Diann Grasse

Staff for DEALING WITH TERMINAL ILLNESS IN THE FAMILY

ASSOCIATE EDITOR Bill Conn
PICTURE RESEARCHER Sarah Bloom
PRODUCTION ASSISTANT Jaimie Winkler
SERIES DESIGNER Takeshi Takahashi
LAYOUT 21st Century Publishing and Communications, Inc.

http://www.chelseahouse.com

First Printing

1 3 5 7 9 8 6 4 2

Library of Congress Cataloging-in-Publication Data

Wagner, Heather Lehr.
  Dealing with terminal illness in the family / by Heather Lehr Wagner.
    p. cm. — (Focus on family matters)
Summary: Discusses what may happen when a family member becomes terminally ill and
how to cope with this situation.
Includes bibliographical references and index.
  ISBN 0-7910-6692-4 (hardback)
  1. Grief in children—Juvenile literature. 2. Bereavement in children—Juvenile literature.
3. Loss (Psychology) in children—Juvenile literature. 4. Parents—Death—Psychological
aspects—Juvenile literature. 5. Brothers and sisters—Death—Psychological aspects—
Juvenile literature. 6. Children and death—Juvenile literature. [1. Terminally ill—Family
relationships. 2. Grief. 3. Death.] I. Title. II. Series.
BF723.G75 W34 2002
155.9'37—dc21
                                                                    2002000347

Contents

Introduction

Marvin Rosen, Ph.D.K
Consulting Editor

B ad things sometimes happen to good people. We've probably all heard that expression. But what happens when the
"good people" are teenagers?

Growing up is stressful and difficult to negotiate. Teenagers
are struggling to becoming independent, trying to cut ties with
their families that they see as restrictive, burdensome, and
unfair. Rather than attempting to connect in new ways with
their parents, they may withdraw. When bad things do happen,
this separation may make the teen feel alone in coping with
difficult and stressful issues.

Focus on Family Matters provides teens with practical information about how to cope when bad things happen to them.
The series deals foremost with feelings—the emotional pain
associated with adversity. Grieving, fear, anger, stress, guilt,
and sadness are addressed head on. Teens will gain valuable
insight and advice about dealing with their feelings, and for
seeking help when they cannot help themselves.

The authors in this series identify some of the more serious
problems teens face. In so doing, they make three assumptions:
First, teens who find themselves in difficult situations are not at
fault and should not blame themselves. Second, teens can over-
come difficult situations, but may need help to do so. Third,
teens bond with their families, and the strength of this bond
influences their ability to handle difficult situations.

These books are also about communication—specifically
about the value of communication. None of the problems
covered occurs in a vacuum, and none of the situations should

be faced by anyone alone. Each either involves a close family member or affects the entire family. Since families teach teens how to trust, relate to others, and solve problems, teens need to bond with families to develop normally and become emotionally whole. Success in dealing with adversity depends not only on the strength of the individual teen, but also upon the resources of the family in providing support, advice, and material assistance. Strong attachment to care givers in a supporting, nurturing, safe family structure is essential to successful coping.

Some teens learn to cope with adversity—they absorb the pain, they adjust, and they go on. But for others, the trauma they experience seems like an insurmountable challenge—they become angry, stressed, and depressed. They may withdraw from friends, they may stop going to school, and their grades may slip. They may draw negative attention to themselves and express their pain and fear by rebelling. Yet, in each case, healing can occur.

The teens who cope well with adversity, who are able to put the past behind them and regain their momentum, are no less sensitive or caring than those who suffer most. Yet there is a difference. Teens who are more resilient to trauma are able to dig deep down into their own resources, to find strength in their families and in their own skills, accomplishments, goals, aspirations, and values. They are able to find reasons for optimism and to feel confidence in their capabilities. This series recognizes the effectiveness of these strategies, and presents problem-solving skills that every teen can use.

Focus on Family Matters is positive, optimistic, and supportive. It gives teens hope and reinforces the power of their own efforts to handle adversity. And most importantly, it shows teens that while they cannot undo the bad things that have happen, they have the power to shape their own futures and flourish as healthy, productive adults.

An End and a Beginning

■ Stephanie can remember a time before her mother's illness, a time when her family was normal. They each had their own activities—her mother and father worked, she and her younger sister went to school and swimming and gymnastics, and occasionally the family would come together for a meal and to talk about what everyone was doing before setting off again to do what they wanted. Everyone was busy, but their family was no different from the other families she knew.

She and her mother had fights sometimes—fights about small things, like her clothes or wearing make-up, or how late she could stay up, or how long she could talk on the telephone. They never fought for too long, and they never stayed angry at each other. Her mother always commented that the argument proved how much her mother loved her. If she didn't care, she would just let Stephanie do whatever she wanted.

Those times of being a normal family are just a memory now, growing more distant with every day. A few months ago,

Stephanie's mother learned that she had ovarian cancer. Their family life has changed so completely that sometimes Stephanie imagines that the cancer is not really inside her mother but is instead in their house, eating away at the life they once had and destroying everything.

Now her mother is focusing on her treatment, on trying to get better. She is weak from the chemotherapy, her hair has fallen out, and she looks like a stranger. Sometimes she barely seems to see Stephanie, let alone notice what she is wearing or how much make-up she has on. The arguments that once proved how much her mother loved her have disappeared. Instead there is silence, or discussions of her mother's illness in whispers and sighs.

For families struggling with **terminal illness**, the disease that has attacked one family member has, in a sense, infected them all. The life they shared is gone, and now, as one family member deals with a life-threatening illness, the others must understand this change and find their place in the new family that will emerge as the disease progresses.

For an illness to be described as **terminal**, it means that this illness is very serious and will, most likely, cause someone to die. The word terminal means final, or coming at the end, and so someone suffering from a terminal illness is probably near the end of his or her life.

What is a terminal illness?

For both the person struggling with a terminal illness and his or her family, the first victim of the illness will be the family's "normal" life. The second will be the dreams they shared—dreams for a future that may never happen.

When terminal illness strikes a brother or sister, or a parent, the rest of the family can feel helpless and alone, ignored by their parents and relatives as everyone focuses

Everyone in the family must deal with the effects of terminal illness when a parent or sibling gets sick, and many times family members must assume new roles to help the family survive when someone dies.

on the person who has become sick. For Stephanie, her mother's illness meant an end to their arguments over clothing and make-up, the "normal" disagreements teens and parents have. Rather than feeling happy to suddenly be allowed to wear whatever she wanted, Stephanie felt sad and even angry with her mother. Her mother had told her that the fights were a sign that her mother cared about her.

How does

terminal illness affect a family?

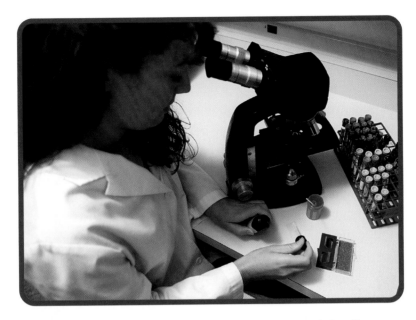

With modern medicine, doctors can treat many of the diseases that were once life-threatening, which is why it is shocking and hard to understand when a loved one is diagnosed with a terminal illness. However, death is a natural part of the life cycle.

Without any more fighting, it was as if her mother cared more about her disease than her daughter.

There are no simple, easy solutions for families battling terminal illness. The struggle they face is a terribly sad one, particularly since it will most likely end in the loss of someone they care about.

The circle of life

It was once much more clearly understood that life was a cycle, that death was a closer and more familiar part of family life. Before modern medicine, disease and death were more visible and common, with few families untouched by the loss of a child or a young parent. Family members who had died were "laid out" in a room in the family house—the parlor or living room or the best space in the home—where friends and family would come to "pay their respects," a visit to comfort the family and honor their loved one who had died.

But in our modern days, death has become unfamiliar. We are living longer, healthier lives. It is generally accepted that we will grow to comfortable old age, surrounded by our grandchildren, before slipping away peacefully and quietly at the end of many happy years. Most of us do not confront death on a daily basis, and those suffering illness are generally treated in hospitals, not in the family's home.

As a result, when a terminal illness strikes, it can feel almost like a failing—a failing of medicine, a failing of the doctors, or even of the patient. We want someone to be responsible—perhaps the sick person smoked, or drank too much, or didn't exercise, or didn't eat properly. It is difficult to accept that serious illness can interrupt a happy life and that this can happen with no reason and no warning.

A family struggling with terminal illness may find that all areas of their life are tested. Work and school may become more difficult. Friends who learn of the illness may disappear, in part because they are not sure what to say or do, in part because the illness is a reminder that all of our lives are fragile, that illness can strike anyone at any time. Family members can drift apart, with parents focusing all their attention on the illness and the loved one struggling with it. Words, arguments, and actions can take on tremendous meaning.

It is normal to feel angry with the person who is sick, particularly if they require a lot of time and energy from parents and other family members. It is normal to want the life "before" (before the illness) back, to want things to return to the way they once were.

Sadly, this cannot happen. There will be beginnings and endings in every family's life, and terminal illness will bring a different kind of ending. But there are ways to deal with terminal illness in your family, to understand your feelings

The emotions family members feel when a loved one has a terminal illness will make living a normal life a challenge. Going to school and work, and maintaining friendships becomes difficult when someone is caring for a sick loved one.

and to find comfort in **grieving** the loss of someone you care about. In the following chapters, we will talk about the stages of sadness you will pass through, the changes your family may experience, and some ways to say goodbye. We will also examine some coping skills that may be useful as you struggle with your own healing.

What does it feel like

when a parent is diagnosed with a terminal illness?

Each life contains many seasons, and in a family there are times of sorrow and times of joy. For families struggling with terminal illness, feelings and emotions can sometimes seem overwhelming. The next chapter will explore these emotions and help you to understand why you feel the way you do.

The Ways
We Grieve

◼ Jack's family life has changed, too. His little brother, David, has been diagnosed with **leukemia**. It is sometimes strange to Jack that a disease with such a frightening name can have found a place inside the body of his tiny brother. A three-year-old shouldn't have to worry about dying. Jack hadn't even had time to teach him to play baseball. He had spent too much of his life in hospitals already.

Jack felt as if the disease had become the most important thing in his family, more important than any one of them as an individual. It had become the focus of his parents' lives—when they weren't in the hospital with David, they were poring over medical books or searching on the Internet, trying to find some information that might make a difference in David's treatment. Jack barely saw his parents anymore. He stayed at school as long as he could, participating in any games that were going on, signing up for every after-school activity, just to avoid going home to an empty house.

His friends didn't know that his little brother was sick, and Jack liked that. They were the only ones who behaved normally. It was the one part of Jack's life that felt the same, untouched by his brother's disease.

Jack had seen what happened when people knew how sick his brother was. His parents' friends either stopped calling and coming by—as if the disease was somehow contagious— or they were there all the time, bringing over food and talking quietly. Then his parents would cry, and Jack felt so helpless. It was if something important—some critical part of their family—had already died.

There are many emotions that touch a family struggling with terminal illness. We all, consciously or unconsciously, plan out our futures, dreaming of a life marked by significant milestones. These milestones may include things like graduations, weddings, the birth of a child, or even the smaller moments that mark the passage of time: a new school year, a dance, a date, a concert, or a football game. We imagine these events, picturing what they will be like and who will be there to share them with us.

We mark the passage of time in other ways as well, with the customs and **rituals** that shape our family life. Cutting down a Christmas tree, decorating the house with birthday balloons, planting spring bulbs or a vegetable garden, carving the Halloween pumpkin—these rituals comfort us because they show that, as seasons change and years go by, certain things remain the same.

These dreams and rituals are often drastically changed when terminal illness strikes a family. Activities that had once been part of the weekly or annual routine can no longer be counted on. A parent may be too ill to

How would you feel

if your parent became too ill to take care of you?

participate, or may need to spend time at the hospital to

It is normal to feel sad and angry, and to deny that a loved one has a terminal illness. Eventually, the family may come to accept the difficulty of the illness, and help the sick person find peace.

care for a sick brother or sister. Significant events may pass without anyone seeming to notice or care.

This loss of dreams and change in comforting rituals and routines is often the first sign that terminal illness has struck a family. A once-bustling house may become quiet or empty. A family whose schedule once revolved around school and sports may now find the calendar occupied by medical appointments and trips to the hospital.

The possibility of a terminal illness ending in the death of a loved one is frightening. The process of death and dying is unfamiliar to most of us, and we may be uncertain how to behave around someone struggling with a serious disease. We may feel uncomfortable, uncertain of what to say, unsure whether or not to mention their illness. Should we talk about other things, things that are positive and happy? Should we deny that they are sick, or should we protect them from bad news and only talk about cheerful things?

It may be helpful to remember that the illness may change the health of someone, but not the essence of who they are as a person. The same brother or sister, father or mother is still there, and while the disease may affect their outward appearance, the life inside has not been altered. If you were battling an illness, you would want to know that your family was fighting with you, not denying that the illness exists. Talking honestly about what is going on, letting them know that you are there, no matter what, can be a truly powerful gift.

But it is important to be honest with yourself, as well. Understanding your emotions and focusing on your feelings first can prepare you to be more supportive of your family member. Grief does not come only after someone has died; grief strikes much earlier, as you begin to understand that someone you care about is very ill and may not survive that illness.

The writer Elisabeth Kübler-Ross identified five stages of grief that most people experience in her book *On Death and Dying*. These five stages are: denial, anger, bargaining, depression, and acceptance. These stages explain the feelings that are most common when a tragedy strikes. While they may not necessarily occur in a neat and predictable order (you may feel depressed one day and angry the next), it is helpful to learn about these stages to better understand your feelings during this time.

How would you react if a member of your family was dealing with a terminal illness?

This can't be happening

The first stage of grief identified by Dr. Kübler-Ross is **denial**. We all have had moments where we've refused to admit that something bad could be happening to us. We hope that we can somehow wish away bad news—that perhaps it's simply a mistake, a mix-up of lab tests, an inexperienced doctor, a diagnosis that will be changed if we simply get a second opinion.

Because of the great success modern medicine has made in prolonging life, we have come to expect that people will live to be 80 years old, or perhaps older. Our expectations for long life make it harder for us to accept a terminal illness in someone young. It is difficult to imagine that a young child, or a previously healthy parent, can suddenly be struggling for their life. "How can they have cancer?" we might ask. "They are too *young*."

We may choose to deny the randomness of terminal illness. As we discussed in the last chapter, we often want there to be an explanation, a cause, of disease. It is difficult to admit that a serious illness can strike not because of, but in spite of, a patient's actions. There may be certain actions people can take—eating a healthy diet, exercising regularly—that will help to fight off disease, but there are no guarantees, no prevention plan to eliminate terminal illness. Part of the fear that terminal illness inspires is its very randomness, the fact that so often there is no explanation and no reason for its appearance in someone who had previously been healthy.

Denial comes when you pretend that everything is okay, that your family life has not changed. It can slip in when you refuse to talk about the illness or its effects on you and your family.

There may be times when you simply don't want to think about the illness, when you need a break from worrying about your loved one and want to escape from the fear hanging over your family. This is normal.

But is important not to refuse to think about what is happening. It is important to understand that you will be afraid of the unknown, and afraid of what you do know. You may worry about your family member, and worry about whether you might become sick, too. Find someone that you

Pretending that terminal illness is not happening to a family member will not make it disappear. It is important to live life as normally as possible when dealing with a terminal illness, but it is equally important to confront the anger and sadness you feel.

can talk to, and share what is happening. Do not feel that you need to "be strong," to handle this on your own. Talk with your friends, a family member, a teacher or counselor.

And be honest with your family as well, particularly with the person suffering from the disease. Don't feel that you have to pretend to be bright and happy if you're worried or sad. By sharing your feelings, you will give them the chance to be honest with you, too, and to let you know how they are feeling. Your honesty will be one of the best gifts you can give them.

Managing anger

Anger is an emotion that makes many people uncomfortable. They are afraid of its intensity, afraid that it will be an emotion that they can't control.

But anger is a normal emotion, one that is to be expected when something tragic happens to you or to someone you

When a loved one is sick, it is normal to feel angry – you may be angry at the unfairness of the situation, at the doctors who don't have a cure, or at your friends who haven't experienced terminal illness. There are ways to manage anger in a healthy way, like keeping a journal or playing sports.

love. When denial finally slips away, when you begin to realize that the illness is not a mistake, you may find yourself becoming very angry. The thought that "this can't be happening to my family" may be replaced by a real anger that it *is*, in fact, happening to a member of your family. You may be overwhelmed by the unfairness of the illness, and things that previously would not have bothered you may now begin to bother you—a lot.

You may feel anger at the doctors who are unable to instantly cure someone you care about. You may feel anger at the people who slip away from your family as the disease progresses. You may become angry with people who, uncertain of what to say, say something thoughtless. You may become angry with people who are healthy, whose lives haven't changed. You may even become angry with the family member who is sick—angry with them for needing so much care and attention, angry with them for becoming sick in the first place.

This anger, particularly when it is directed at the person who is sick, can be truly frightening. Understand that it is normal to want things to be the way they were, and to feel angry that your life has changed. There are things that you can do to help manage your anger, safe ways that you can release this strong emotion.

One way to manage anger is to write it out. Keep a journal, and write in it when you are feeling angry or upset. Putting your feelings down on paper will help you to better understand the circumstances and situations that are the most difficult for you, and also will give you a safe place to let go of those strong emotions.

How would you deal

with your anger if a family member was diagnosed with a terminal illness?

Anger can create a tremendous amount of energy. You want to be able to direct that energy into a positive, rather than negative, force. In addition to releasing your anger by writing it down, you may find that physical activities are a positive outlet for strong emotions. Sports are a great way to channel energy, whether you choose a team sport like football, soccer, or field hockey, or an individual activity like jogging or rollerblading. Even a brisk walk or a bike ride can help clear out your anger, giving you a way to manage your feelings rather than having them manage you.

Nothing to negotiate

We all have had moments where we tried to bargain our way out of a bad situation, attempting to "cut a deal" by offering up something important in the hope of getting something even more important. When terminal illness strikes someone in our family, we may find ourselves offering up frantic prayers, saying something like, "I promise I will never have another mean thought about my mother, if only she will be okay."

This is known as **bargaining**. But while bargaining may work in other aspects of life (promising to do your sister's chores for a week if she'll lend you her jacket), the disease's progress rarely responds to our promises of good deeds or kind thoughts. It is yet another sign of the randomness of the disease that it cannot respond to our wishes or demands.

Understanding that bargaining cannot work is part of the

grieving process. It requires you to admit that you are helpless. Many of us grow up with the belief that we can do almost anything if we work hard enough or practice often enough.

But when terminal illness strikes someone we care about, we come face to face with the realization that there are some things we can't fix. Medicine is capable of great works of healing, but there are some diseases so powerful that doctors cannot cure them. It is not a matter of finding the right doctor, the right hospital, or the right treatment.

How would you feel if there was nothing you could do to fight a family member's terminal illness?

Part of the growing up process involves this important understanding. As young children, we believe that the world revolves around us, that our family, school and friends exist in relation to us. As we grow older, we begin to understand that friends, parents, teachers, all have a life separate and apart from our own. We also begin to understand that we are not all-powerful, that our thoughts and actions do not cause something to happen or not to happen.

While you will not be able to change the disease's progress through good deeds or being a better person, there is something to be gained from the understanding that the arguments that once seemed so important matter little in life. Perhaps the most valuable gift terminal illness presents is the understanding that life is precious, that each moment counts. As you wrestle with the prospect of losing someone you care about, remember that there are small ways you can make a difference—ways that will not change the health of your loved one but will make the end of their life easier. Be honest with them, and with yourself. Do not be afraid to talk about their illness, or to share how much you will miss them. Spend time with them—cherish their presence in your life.

Dealing with depression

The fourth stage of the grieving process is **depression**. Most of us have experienced this emotion at one time or another. There is no mystery here—it is normal and natural to feel sadness at the prospect of losing someone important to you, someone you love and care about. It would be foolish to pretend that everything is ok, that the illness does not matter. It is important to allow yourself to feel this sadness, to admit that your life has changed.

Depression can be an overwhelming emotion, making you feel helpless. The danger of depression is its ability to blot out energy, happiness, and

Depression can be overwhelming if you try to handle it by yourself. Friends are a valuable resource when dealing with depression, and can help you cope with a terminal illness by providing support and relief from some of the stress and sadness.

hope. The key to managing depression is to understand that it will end, and that the huge sadness and bleakness you feel is part of a stage, a normal product of grief. Understanding this will help you to remember, when the sadness comes, that it will not last forever.

The first and best thing you can do to battle depression is to force yourself to keep moving, to continue to do the things that normally make you happy, even when you don't want to. Be active; do not allow depression to shut you up in your room, away from your family and friends. If you enjoy being outdoors, go outside for a walk or a run. If you feel better with friends, call them and arrange to meet somewhere. The important thing is to hold on to the things that make you happy and continue to do them, even when your energy level is low.

Sometimes, when a family member is struggling with a disease, we feel a responsibility to spend every minute with them, because each moment is precious. But helping to care for someone who is struggling with a disease can be an exhausting and depressing task. Give yourself permission to take a break from time to time. Give yourself permission to continue living. Continue to participate in whatever gives you pleasure, whether it's after-school sports, a dance class, or a trip to the mall with friends. Remember that it is all right to want a break from time to time. By taking care of yourself, you will find that you have more energy for your family, and feel stronger.

Finding peace

The goal for family members struggling with a loved one's terminal illness is to reach a point where the reality of the illness, the limited amount of time remaining in his or her life, is openly admitted and understood. Dr. Kübler-Ross refers to this stage in the grieving process as **acceptance**. Accepting the reality of the terminal illness, and the changes it will bring, does not mean feeling good about it or not hoping for a miraculous cure. It simply means understanding that your father or mother, sister or brother, is battling a life-threatening illness and that there is a chance they will not win that battle.

It is not easy to reach the point where you admit that the illness may be more powerful than doctors or any force you can call upon. Many times, it is the ill family member who will reach the stage of acceptance before the rest of the family does. They may have a better sense of the course of their illness, whether from talking to doctors and nurses or simply as part of the body's process of preparing for death.

The sick family member may even want to discuss this prospect with you, to share their sense that time is limited. A critically ill parent may want to talk to you about his or her future hopes and dreams for your life, give you advice

Part of the grieving process involves the acceptance of the reality of the terminal illness. By discussing the terminal illness, both you and your sick loved one may find peace in the limited time you have left together.

about school or dating or marriage, discuss their wishes for a funeral or for the final stages of their care. It is important not to dismiss them or discourage them by saying things like, "Oh, don't talk like that. You're not that sick." It may be quite difficult to hear someone you care about admit that they are ready to die, particularly if you do not

What would you do

if a family member wanted to talk to you about their death?

feel ready to let them go. Understand that they are passing through the stages of grief, just as you are, and yet their path will be different and their progress may be faster or slower.

For those whose loved one is dying, the greatest challenge can be not to cling tightly, but to share their end gently, letting them know that you will be there but not hold them back when they are ready to go. Be prepared to feel many different emotions. Understand that grief will not be quick or temporary, but will last a while as you pass through many different stages of saying good-bye.

Portraits of Sorrow

■ For Megan, the news that her grandmother had been hospitalized was not upsetting. Her grandmother had had several minor medical problems over the years, and had been hospitalized for back surgery and for an eye operation, emerging more energetic and healthier than ever.

But this time was different. Megan had returned from school one afternoon to find that her parents had left work early. They shared the news that her grandmother had been diagnosed with cancer, and that the disease had advanced to a stage that the doctors were offering little hope for a recovery.

Megan's first visit to the hospital brought a shock. "Suddenly, my grandmother looked old. She always looked so elegant, always had her hair done and wore the most beautiful jewelry. And in the hospital bed, she was just lying there, her hair all messy and in this hospital gown. She looked like an old woman. I had never thought about her that way before."

Hospitals can be an unfamiliar and uncomfortable setting, with their sterile smells and brisk approach to illness. But they can also offer a kind of false promise. Hospitals are places of healing. We expect hospital stays to lead to recovery, to doctors "making things better." It can be even harder to accept that an illness is terminal when a loved one is surrounded by experienced and professional medical caregivers.

The doctors had been honest with Megan's grandmother, sharing their opinion that the cancer was progressing rapidly and that the prospects for her complete recovery were very small. Megan's grandmother chose not to pursue aggressive treatment, not to undergo some of the options available to her—extensive surgery followed by radiation or **chemotherapy**. This, too, was particularly difficult for Megan to understand.

"It made me angry when I heard my parents say that Grandma had decided not to have the surgery," Megan shared. "I couldn't believe that she wouldn't want to try anything. If it was me, I could take every chance I had, every possible treatment. Every month is precious. I would want to live for as long as I possibly could. I would try surgery, a macrobiotic diet, even the radiation that makes your hair fall out. I would try everything I could."

What challenged Megan about her grandmother's illness was her seeming acceptance of it, her unwillingness to fight for every last month of life. What seemed like a peaceful acceptance of the diagnosis of a terminal illness was, of course, not as simple as it appeared, and Megan later learned that her grandmother had sought the opinions and advice of several different doctors and spent many long hours discussing options with her children before reaching a decision about how she would like to spend her remaining months of life.

It is difficult to learn that someone we love has a terminal illness. Even when the sick person is older and has lived a full life, the illness and the impending loss are always a shock.

Megan's grandmother was fortunate that her circumstances and finances permitted her to choose to be cared for at home. A trained nurse or aide came daily to assist her with tasks as she grew weaker, and to give her medicine to help manage her pain. Megan's family lived close by, and they would visit with her often during the last days of her life.

"At first, I didn't want to see her," Megan said. "I was angry at the cancer and angry at her for not fighting harder.

But then I changed my mind—and all because of a dream. I had a dream that I was at the beach with my grandmother. When we were little and my grandfather was still alive, they would rent a house at the beach and we would spend a week there. Every morning, before breakfast, my grandmother and I would walk to the beach and look for a perfect seashell. We would walk and walk until we found one that we both liked, and then we would go back home. For some reason, one night I had this dream that my grandmother and I were walking along the sand looking for seashells. When I woke up, I just knew that I had to go and see her."

The time Megan spent with her dying grandmother was not always easy. Her grandmother was sometimes in pain, or tired, and so Megan would only stay for a short while. But there were often good days, too, where Megan would talk about what she was doing at school or they would simply sit quietly, looking at pictures and laughing over shared memories. For Megan, there was always a real sadness

What would you do

if someone you loved was dying?

after those visits, as she understood that there were few of them left. Her friends, many of whom had never known their grandparents, did not always understand her sadness.

But for Megan, the prospect of saying goodbye to her grandmother was not made easier because this woman she loved was older. She felt sad that it was only since her grandmother's illness that she had come to truly appreciate how much their relationship mattered to her, and how much she would miss her when she was gone.

Megan's grandmother lived only four months after the terminal illness was first diagnosed. Even two years later, Megan would cry when she remembered her grandmother.

"After she died," Megan said, "my parents and I went through her house, packing things up and deciding what to keep and what to give away. In her attic, we found a glass jar, filled with seashells. They were the shells that she and I had collected during those summers long ago. I think that was the moment when I most missed my grandmother—I realized that nobody else could ever share that memory with me, and that I would never get another chance to do that with her. I have that jar of shells in my room now, and whenever I look at it I think about my grandmother."

For Megan, it did not matter that her grandmother had lived a rich and full life. She wanted more time, a chance to add to the memories they already shared. But Megan found some comfort in the fact that they had been able to spend time together at the end, saying their good-byes not directly but by simply being together, sharing and cherishing those last days as the precious gift that they were.

The experience of grief is specific and individual. We all feel loss differently, and losing someone we care about is a painful process. It is tempting to give in to the "if onlys"—"if only she was older," or "if only this had happened after I was an adult," or any of the other phrases we use to show that a terminal illness is fine if it happens to someone else, or if we could just schedule it at a better time.

There is never an easy time for terminal illness to strike someone in your family, nor is there ever an easy time to watch someone you love die. Adults whose elderly parents are in the final stages of life often experience a great sense of grief and loss, not because their parent has not had a full life but for the simple reason that they must say good-bye to someone important to them. Our parents, our grandparents, our brothers and sisters hold unique memories of who we were, as well as who we are now. They have shared our life with us, often from its earliest moments, and as a result they are a part of how we define

When someone loses a family member to terminal illness, they often feel like they have lost a part of themselves as well. It is never easy to lose a loved one, even if that person has lived a long and happy life.

ourselves: "I am Sue's daughter." "I have two brothers and one sister." "I am Jack's grandson." In a way, as we prepare to say good-bye to a family member, it can feel as if we are saying good-bye to a part of ourselves.

As the next stories show, there is never a good time to

lose a family member. The grief we feel, whether terminal illness has struck a grandparent, a parent, or a brother or sister, is sharp and real.

The words for good-bye

The first sign of Brad's father's illness was a series of headaches that aspirin couldn't seem to erase. He went to his doctor thinking that the stresses of his job were giving him migraines, and found out instead that he had a brain tumor. By the time it was discovered, the tumor had grown so large that it was **inoperable**.

Brad and his sister did not learn of their father's illness immediately. The diagnosis was made in November, and his parents decided not to tell their children until after the holidays, so that their children could enjoy one last Christmas unburdened by the knowledge that it would be their last together as a family.

How would you feel

if your mom or dad waited to tell you about their terminal illness?

But of course it was clear that something was wrong. Brad found his mother crying as she was writing out Christmas cards, and twice that December his father lost his balance and fell, blaming one too many glasses of eggnog. His parents were clearly worried about something, and Brad thought that possibly they were getting a divorce. That was what he was prepared to hear when his parents finally sat down and told their children the news they had held back to avoid spoiling the holiday.

"I couldn't believe it," Brad said. "I thought they were going to talk about the end of their marriage, not the end of my dad's life. He was only 40 years old. How could he be dying? It didn't make sense. He looked the same. I thought that there should be some sort of sign if the tumor was so big that they couldn't operate on it or

One of the most difficult aspects of terminal illness is that it may strike quickly and be very painful for the sick person. It often leaves little time for family members to prepare for life without their loved one.

radiate it. He just looked tired. Not sick. Not dying."

But the signs of the illness's progress soon became clearer. His father lost his balance more often, and then began to find it difficult to walk, shuffling his feet or dragging one foot behind him. His father, an athletic man, had been proud of Brad's success on the soccer team and had attended every game. But as it became harder for him to walk, he stopped being a regular presence along the sidelines.

The brain tumor also took a toll on his father's vision, first causing it to blur and then to nearly disappear. "It felt as if this disease took my dad away in pieces," Brad recalled. "That almost made it more awful. It had to really break him down—take away his ability to walk and then his ability to see—before it killed him."

Brad's strongest memory of his father's illness is of the anger he felt as his father neared the end of his life. That anger is still waiting, beneath the surface, and his memories are full of it. One year after his father's death, he is still struggling with this strong emotion.

"I feel angry at the disease," he said. "For the way it took him away piece by piece. I feel mad at the doctors for not at least trying to operate—it might have helped him. We'll never know now. I even feel mad at my mom and dad for not telling us as soon as they found out. My dad didn't have long to live. There were a few extra weeks there that we could have spent making plans or talking about things. Right now, every extra week feels like it would have made a difference."

Brad is still working through the grieving process, mourning the loss of a man whose illness claimed him quickly and cruelly. His father's final days were spent in a hospital, surrounded by doctors and nurses, or other family members and friends. There was little privacy, and neither Brad nor his father felt comfortable talking about what was really happening. There were no easy words for good-bye, and so they spent their last times together in silence.

Snow angels

For Kelly, the winter months were the time she most missed her little sister, Jessica. Jessica had been diagnosed with leukemia when she was four years old, and the last year of her life had changed Kelly's family forever. Her parents had once been cheerful and happy people, but since Jessica's illness and death, the life they once knew as a family was gone. Kelly remembered the last year of Jessica's life as a time spent with other people's parents. Her parents were either working or at the hospital,

> **How would it feel**
>
> **to spend a long period of time in a hospital?**

and so Kelly went home after school with friends and stayed there until late at night, sometimes even overnight. When she would see her mother or father, they would be stressed from the hospital, worried about Jessica, guilty at leaving her alone—even for a few hours. They didn't seem to realize that Kelly missed them, too. They seldom remembered to ask Kelly about school; they missed the class play and didn't even know about her solo in the fall concert until after it had happened.

There were times when Kelly had hated her little sister for all of the attention she was getting, just for being sick. Kelly had only been eight years old; she hadn't realized how truly sick Jessica was until she came home from the hospital for Christmas. Covered with bandages, being pushed around in a wheelchair, her little sister looked almost like a ghost.

The weather had been warm until January, and then a sudden snow came. Jessica had always loved to play in the snow, but she was too sick to go outside. So Kelly had pushed her wheelchair to the window, and then gone outside and built a snowman facing the window. Just before coming inside, Kelly had pretended to fall backwards in the snow, and then made two snow angels, one for her and one for Jessica. Jessica had loved those pictures in the snow, and stayed close by the window until it grew dark. She had died suddenly only a few days later, still at home.

A family is always devastated when a terminal illness afflicts one of its
members, but it is especially shocking when the victim is a young child.
It is impossible not to think about the long life that child should have lived.

Five years later, her family still carried the scars from Jessica's death. Her parents had stopped laughing, and then stopped talking to each other. They had decided to divorce three years after Jessica died. It was as if they somehow blamed each other for what had happened. Kelly had lost not only her sister, but in a sense, her whole family. She lived with her mother now, and with the first snowfall of each winter she would go out and make snow angels, and remember Jessica.

Changes in the Family

■ Mark had just started his freshman year in high school. During dinner one night, his mom and dad told him that they had some important news to tell him and his little brother, and from the look on his parents faces Mark knew that the news wasn't going to be good. Mark's mother had breast cancer.

As a first step in her treatment, Mark's mother had surgery to remove the cancerous lump in her breast. She was in a lot of pain when she came home from the hospital, and the rest of the family pitched in to make sure she had time to rest and heal. Their lives didn't change much at first—Mark still played basketball after school, and sometimes his mom even picked him up after practice. Some of Mark's anxiety passed, and he thought things were going to get better.

But after his mom had more tests, the doctors told the family that they hadn't caught all of the cancer in time. It had spread to her lymph nodes. There would be chemotherapy and radiation treatments, and the chances of survival were not high.

Mark's life changed drastically. His parents were often at the hospital, and Mark had to miss most basketball practices to babysit his little brother. Eventually, Mark's grandmother moved in to help out, and everything changed – different meals, curfews, and schedules. Mark did his best to adjust, since he knew this was the best way to help his mom.

Terminal illness can affect a family in a number of ways—some clear, some more subtle. With each stage of the illness comes another wave of adjustments, requiring all of the family members to alter their perspective on what is happening, their view of their role in the family, and their expectations of other family members.

This constant state of change can leave you with a sense that the illness has struck each member of the family, one physically and the rest emotionally. When a tragic event happens, we most desperately need the support of our family— their encouragement, their love, their reassurance. But when the tragic event is happening to someone in the family, the others are often focused on the one who is sick. Parents may focus almost exclusively on a sick child, taking care of their needs, spending time with them in the hospital, meeting with doctors and researching treatment options. It may be difficult for them to gather up a lot of additional energy for their other child or children.

What would change if your brother or sister became terminally ill?

When it is a parent who is facing a terminal illness, the challenge to the family is equally great. A parent fighting a serious illness will often be tired and weak, physically unable to participate in many of the activities they previously enjoyed. They may be hospitalized and unable to care for their children. Both parents may be focused on the future— uncertain though it may be—and less aware of the day-to-day events of their family.

New responsibilities

When a parent or child becomes seriously ill, parents may expect more of their older children. They may rely on them to take care of themselves or younger brothers and sisters. Teens may be asked to prepare their own meals, to spend more time on their own, or to arrange their own transportation to and from after-school activities. They may be asked to give up their own plans in order to stay home with younger children, or to help care for the sick parent or spend time with a brother or sister in the hospital

While it is important to remember what a gift this kind of help can be, it can feel like a heavy burden at times. It is important for parents to remember that their children *are* still children. While it is fine to try to fill in when your parents are unable to do everything, it is important not to try to take over the parenting job. If it is your parent who is sick, it may make them feel even more helpless to know that you are doing a job that they feel they should be doing.

So where do you draw the line? Where does "helping out more" slip into "taking over"? Doing your chores or homework without being reminded is a way of helping. And taking care of younger brothers or sisters a few afternoons a week when a parent is unable to, or helping with laundry or setting the table, can be a great assistance to a tired or sick

How would you feel if you had to give up activities because someone in your family was very sick?

When a loved one dies, the other members of the family must assume new roles. A teenager may be given the responsibility of caring for younger siblings, and a father may have to raise his children on his own.

parent. But trying to discipline younger brothers or sisters, creating a new set of household rules, or giving up all of the things you enjoy doing to fill in for absent parents will create problems, both within the family and, more specifically, for you.

It is important to remember that your life is precious and valuable, too. It should not end simply because a loved one is battling a terrible illness. Remember that depression can quickly slip in if you allow yourself to give up all the things that make you happy. You must give yourself permission to have fun, to do something you enjoy. Set aside some time each week for an activity you enjoy and make sure that your parents know of your plans in advance. If they are relying on you to babysit, you may want to ask a friend or relative to take over babysitting for the time that you have soccer practice or want to get together with friends, and let your parents know who will be at home during that time.

Dollars and sense

When a parent suffers a terminal illness, the family may suffer financially as well as emotionally. The parent may no longer be able to work, and if he or she provides the majority of the income for the family, their illness and death may require the family to make major life changes at a time when they are already suffering great loss. The family's home may need to be given up, the remaining parent may need to take a job or work additional hours. Plans for vacations, for college, or for other activities may need to be postponed or given up as the family struggles to make ends meet.

There will be an added sense of loss if much of what is comfortable and familiar is lost in the aftermath of the death of a loved one. If changing financial circumstances require a move or a new school, you will find yourself dealing with very strong feelings.

The sadness involved in losing a member of your family is generally a new and unfamiliar emotion. Part of the grieving and, ultimately, the healing process, is not simply waiting for that sadness to disappear but, instead, learning to live with it, to feel it and yet continue living.

The suffering caused by terminal illness often extends beyond the physical: the family may have to deal with the financial burden created by mounting medical bills and a sick parent's unemployment.

When a major change follows the death of a loved one, this sadness can become even greater. A move can feel as if you are leaving the loved one behind. Small children often question whether the family member who has died will be able to find them if they move. While we understand that moving away from the family's home does not mean moving away from the memories it held, it can be particularly difficult to move after this kind of loss. Changing homes and changing schools can mean leaving understanding friends behind.

What would you do

if the illness or death of a parent meant you had to move or change schools?

If a move is necessary for your family, try to keep some small things that will make you feel more comfortable in a new place. It may be a picture of your home, or of friends. Or you may find it comforting to continue a routine you had before this major change—perhaps you would play basketball every Saturday, or watch your favorite football team on Sunday afternoons. Try to preserve as much of your old routine as possible to guide you through the change and make this new place feel more familiar.

Stay in touch with old friends as much as possible. Send e-mail messages, make phone calls, visit whenever possible. Do not cut yourself off from an important support group just when you need it most.

The missing piece

When a loved one dies following a terminal illness, it can feel as if the family is a puzzle with one central piece missing. Bit by bit, the other family members may struggle to bridge the gap left by the missing person, trying to fill in the empty space left in their midst. Grief can make this a painful process. It is not a matter of forgetting, but rather an effort to continue to be a family, only a family with one less person in it.

There are simple dynamics that make up a family structure, and the death of one family member can completely change the group as a whole and each person's role in it. The death of a father can leave his wife newly defined as a "single mother," with new responsibilities for supporting and caring for her family on her own. A stay-at-home mom may now need to find a job and may be less available for her children.

When a brother or sister dies, the children in the family may find themselves in a different position. The death of a sibling may mean that you will become an

When a loved one dies, it may feel like there is a piece missing in the family puzzle. Although the hole left by the death of a family member will never be filled, spending time together and sharing activities can help the family survive.

only child, or the oldest, or the youngest, or the only brother or sister in the family. You may find yourself behaving differently to "fit" this new definition, or to distract your parents from their grief.

The description of a family as a puzzle is a valid one in many ways. No one piece can replace another, nor can a piece be removed without the picture feeling incomplete. The grieving process will take time. Respect the important

How would it feel

to change your position in the family—from youngest child to only child, or from middle child to oldest?

Normal activities like school become difficult during times of sorrow. When a family member dies, school counselors and other trusted adults can help you deal with your grief.

part each member played in your family. Do not rush to fill up the gaps your loved one's death will leave behind.

Sharing and caring

Even if you are not forced to confront a major change like a move, the loss of a loved one following a terminal illness can feel as if you've been placed in an unfamiliar environment. If the illness was a long one, much of your family's life may have revolved around hospital visits, medical treatments, and efforts to care for someone who was very ill. The absence of this routine can leave a hole, with family members unsure of how to revert back to what they had done to fill their days before the illness began.

School can be a real challenge during this time of grieving. It may be difficult to relate to friends or other students who have not experienced what you have. The concerns of your friends—the daily gossip of school life, relationships and troubles with teachers or parents—may feel trivial to you. It may feel as if you've changed so drastically that what once was familiar and comfortable is now completely alien.

It is important to remember that there are others who can share your feelings, others who have lost a parent or a brother or sister. Talk with a school counselor, a teacher, or minister, priest or other spiritual leader. Ask them to recommend a support group. Some may be listed in the yellow pages of your phone book or in your local newspaper. You will find others on the web. Some useful resources and sources of support are also listed at the back of this book.

Saying Good-bye

■ Donna was afraid to go into her father's bedroom after the doctors sent him home because they could do nothing more to fight his lung cancer. Every time she saw him, his ventilator, and the other medical supplies from the hospital, she felt like crying. She didn't want to upset her father, so she acted brave.

One afternoon when Donna brought her father a glass of water, he told her that he was going to miss her. Donna immediately felt the tears welling up in her eyes, and when she looked at her father, he was already crying. They had both been trying to be strong for each other, and it was such a relief to let out their emotions. Donna told her father everything she wanted to—how scared and sad she was, how much she loved him, and even how much she would miss him. Her father told her that he would miss her too, but that he had lived a good life, and would leave this world knowing that he had raised a strong and smart daughter.

Donna never hesitated to go into her father's bedroom after that day, and they spent a lot of time together watching their favorite TV shows and talking. When he did die, Donna was sad—but she was also happy that she shared her feelings with her father before it was too late.

During the final stage of terminal illness, we are called upon to do something we dread: saying good-bye to someone we love. As the illness changes our family member in visible and invisible ways, it can seem easier to cling to what is familiar, to hold on to the present and not face the future.

But the process of openly and honestly discussing death can be very healing. It is important for our sick parent, brother or sister, or grandparent to understand that they are loved and will be missed. A sudden, unexpected death of a family member often leaves many regrets among those who have survived, and the phrase, "Oh, if only I had told them how much they meant to me" is painfully familiar to those who have suffered a tragic loss. It is difficult to think of terminal illness in any kind of positive light, but one of the gifts it does provide is the knowledge that death is a strong possibility and the need to make the most of each moment. While each of us is vaguely aware that our family members will not live forever, a diagnosis of a terminal illness often puts a more specific deadline on the time left, measured sometimes in years rather than decades, or months rather than years.

It is important not to waste this one gift—the opportunity to let someone know, specifically and clearly, how much they mean to you. Do not be afraid of upsetting them, or yourself. Death is sad, and tears are often the only right response. Often the person who is sick will not discuss their

What would you say to your mother or father if you knew they were dying?

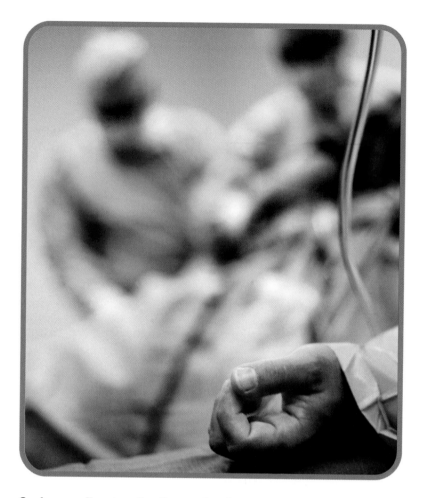

Saying goodbye to a family member is one of the most difficult aspects of dealing with a terminal illness. However, living with the regret of having missed the opportunity to express your love for a dying family member is even worse.

illness for fear of upsetting the rest of the family, while the rest of the family maintains a total silence for fear of upsetting the person who is sick!

Be honest—with yourself and the rest of your family. Admit that you are sad. Admit that you will miss your mother or father, your sister or brother. Speak to them about the illness. Let them know that you will be with them for this last part of their life's journey, and that they don't need to pretend with you that everything is okay. Share your memories. Cry together. Give them the gift of your support, your love—and your true feelings.

A time to mourn

In olden days, there were clear rules to govern the behavior of family members after a loved one's death. Black clothing was worn to show friends and strangers that you were in mourning. You were not expected to immediately resume your regular life until a fixed period of time had passed. Friends and relatives came to your house to call upon you and offer support. In cities, dirt would often be scattered on the street outside the home to muffle the sound of carriages passing by, so that grieving families would not need to be reminded that life was continuing as normal outside their door.

Today, many of the rituals and customs of mourning have changed. There is no specific article of clothing that signals our loss to the world. We are often expected to go on with our lives, to "put the past behind us," by well-meaning friends.

But the process of feeling sad, of admitting that we have lost something important, is a critical step in the healing process. There is no specific timeframe for feeling a less intense kind of sadness.

When a loved one dies, it is during the funeral that friends and family members gather around to offer their support and share the pain of the loss. The thought of a funeral, with its unfamiliar ceremonies and rituals, can be frightening. Parents may sometimes feel that young children should not attend a funeral because it may be too painful for them. But it is often an important part of the

Why is it important

to have a funeral or other ceremony after someone has died?

grieving process. A loss has happened; a death has taken place. Funerals can be the most public sign that a family has suffered a significant loss. By seeing the casket or the urn, the death becomes visible and more real. By sharing memories and tears, family members can begin the healing process.

In Jewish tradition, mourning is not merely expected—it is an obligation, a kind of duty to the one who died. The period of mourning, known as shiva, is expected to last seven days.

In Muslim countries, a death is quickly followed by a funeral and burial, often within a single day. The body will be dressed in a special garment, called a shroud, and then carried through the streets. Male family members and friends will walk before and behind the body, and strangers will often join the procession as it passes through the streets. It is considered to be a good deed to share in the sorrow of death, even if you did not personally know the dead person or his or her family. Specific dates are set aside for visits to the grave after burial, and the period of mourning generally lasts 40 days.

We can even look to history to better understand the importance ancient cultures placed on rituals and traditions marking a death. The pyramids that still stand were originally constructed as a monument to honor the pharaohs who ruled Egypt and as a place to house their tombs. In ancient Egypt, death was viewed as a beginning rather than an ending—the beginning of a journey to another, better world. Furniture, jewels and other luxuries were buried in the tomb, so that the pharaoh would have all the comforts of this world with him in the next.

Hints of this same tradition continue today, as loved ones are often buried with particular significant objects. Perhaps they may be wearing a favorite dress or suit, or be buried with a cherished stuffed animal or a baseball glove. These

There are many traditions and religious ceremonies that surround death that help the living say goodbye to their loved ones. The pyramids in Egypt were built as tombs for the pharaohs, and housed everything that would be needed for a comfortable journey into the afterlife.

are all ways to show that death took not a body but a real person with dreams and joys.

Different faiths offer different perspectives on death and on the rituals that go with it. Whether funerals, ceremonies by the gravesite, or a small service of remembrance, these traditions can provide a rare opportunity for the community to come together to show their support and share their sense of loss.

Life After Death

■ It had been almost a year since Jen's brother had died, and she was starting to feel more like herself. At first, the only memories she had of John were of him being sick – the bald head, bloated face, and skinny arms and legs his chemotherapy created. But after talking to the school counselor, and after some time had past, things started to get better. The memories of the sick John were gradually replaced by happier images, like the two of them swimming together at the lake during the summer.

Jen also felt guilty about enjoying herself. She had decided to skip the school prom that was a few months after John's death, and was even thinking about quitting the volleyball team. She didn't want to enjoy all these things if John never would.

But Jen's mom made her go to the dance, and made her stay on the volleyball team. She asked Jen if she really thought that her brother would want her to stop living her life, to never have fun again. And the more Jen thought about it, the more she knew her mother was right. John would want her to be happy, and would be hurt if she wasn't.

Everyone grieves in different ways and for different lengths of time. The pain caused by a family member's illness and death will eventually fade, and give rise to happy memories about their life.

It is impossible to measure the healing process in terms of weeks or months or even years. There is no fixed timetable to feeling better after a great loss. It is important to give yourself time to feel pain before you can expect to heal. The memories of your family member's illness will begin to fade, and instead be replaced by more complete memories, of a life rich with many happy moments. The gift of healing comes not when you can forget, but when the memories you hold contain the full spectrum of your loved one's life, not merely its sad ending.

There will be a life after the death of a loved one, both for you and your family. The challenge is to live it fully, not ignoring the pain of your loss but admitting it and then moving on. By continuing to live your life, by finding moments of happiness and pleasure, you are not being disloyal to the memory of your family member who has died. Instead, you are honoring them by not allowing their absence to cripple you.

Keep active. Work out your emotions through exercise or sports. Take a walk or a run. Do not give in to the temptation to hide away in a dark place. Keep moving, keep to a routine and stay involved in school and other activities.

The promise of this book is that healing *will* come, with time. There will be moments when you will feel sad or depressed, and others when you will feel angry. Deal with these emotions openly, as we have discussed earlier in this book. Share your feelings with a friend, a family

How long does it take

to heal after the death of someone you love?

member, or a counselor. Write them down in a journal. Even write a letter to the family member who has died, letting them know that you miss them.

Art can provide another outlet for your emotions. If you find it easier to draw than write, try capturing your feelings in a painting or a picture drawn with colored pencils. Counselors refer to this as "art therapy," and the act of expressing your feelings creatively can be a great way to continue to heal.

How would you express

your feelings of sadness and grief?

Music is another way to express your emotions creatively. You may enjoy singing or playing an instrument. Look for a piece of music or song that expresses your feelings, or write one yourself.

In addition to the things you can do to deal with your feelings, it can be helpful to find an additional source of support. There are many networks for teens dealing with grief and depression. Ask an adult to help you find a counselor who will be trained to help you manage these emotions. Schools, churches, hospitals and other local organizations often host meetings for families who have lost a family member to terminal illness. The phone book, or your local newspaper, may also list support groups who can help with specific issues surrounding your loss. There are even camps, such as Camp Good Grief, that provide a summer retreat for teens who have lost a parent, grandparent, brother or sister.

The Internet is another excellent place to search for information and national support groups that may be helpful, both in providing additional resources and in linking you up with local chapters that can offer counseling and peer networks. Organizations such as The Compassionate Friends, Inc., specialize in the issues facing parents who have lost a child or teens who have lost a brother or sister. The U.S. government's National Health Information Center *(www.health.gov/nhic/)* provides a valuable on-line database with links to many different organizations offering specific support for patients and their families dealing with many different illnesses. The web site *www.griefnet.org* offers another forum for sharing your feelings with others who have suffered similar losses. There are additional on-line resources listed at the back of this book.

A day of remembrance

For many who have lost a family member, certain days trigger a greater amount of grief and sorrow. Holidays, anniversaries, and birthdays can all bring back memories.

Holidays and significant events are often touched by sadness after a loved one's death. Choosing a day to celebrate the loved one's life can help keep happy memories of them fresh in your mind.

The day a family member died can become another sadly significant date.

As we have discussed, grief is not something to be smothered, and memories should not be covered up. The goal is to remember special people in our lives with love, reflecting on happy memories and not being afraid to cry when we feel once more the pain of their absence.

One idea is to create a Day of Remembrance—a day when you will honor the family member who has died. You may choose to celebrate this day on their birthday, or on a particular holiday, or on some other day that has special meaning for you and your family. Many families find it helpful to celebrate this day together with a special dinner, or by lighting a candle, by releasing balloons or looking at pictures. There are no right or wrong ways to remember someone who has died. Look back with love, laughter and tears, and remember that the illness that claimed the physical body of someone you loved did not take away their spirit, or the memories they left behind.

A new life

You will honor the memory of your loved one most by going on with your life. With change, even change brought about from sadness, comes growth. You can continue to find purpose in each day by maintaining the routines that shape your life—school, sports, activities, even summer jobs and household chores can provide a framework for this new chapter.

You may find yourself, as you grow older, pursuing particular subjects in school, or thinking about a particular career, as a kind of tribute to the relative who has died. You may want to begin to compile a scrapbook of your own memories, to share them with other relatives or even the family of your own you will one day have. Some choose to name a new baby

> **What would you do**
>
> **to honor the memory of a family member who has died after an illness?**

after the relative who died, not as a way to replace them, but instead as a sign that the cycle of life continues endlessly and that grief and joy do not need to exist separately

It is important to continue with your life after the death of a loved one, and to accept the change that their death has brought to your life. By doing so, you will grow and honor their memory most by being successful and happy.

from each other but instead can blend together in new life and new growth.

Remember that healing does not mean forgetting. Do not be afraid that, as your grief grows less sharp, as you find yourself smiling or laughing one day, you are somehow being disloyal to the person who has died. You will not forget them. But, with time and some hard work, you will find that your memories are of a well-loved person, not an illness.

Glossary

Acceptance – admitting and understanding the reality of a terrible situation like terminal illness; the final stage in the grieving process.

Bargaining – offering something important (like a prayer) in the hope of receiving something more important (like a cure for illness) in return; one of the stages in the grieving process.

Chemotherapy – the use of chemicals to fight diseases like cancer.

Denial – the refusal to believe that something bad like a terminal illness is actually happening; the first stage in the grieving process.

Depression – a feeling of deep and lasting sadness that can rob you of energy and enthusiasm; one of the stages in the grieving process.

Inoperable – a condition, like certain tumors, that cannot be treated with surgery.

Leukemia – a disease that causes an increase in the number of white blood cells in the body.

Rituals – customs and traditions that mark the passage of time.

Terminal – the end of something.

Terminal illness – an illness that will most likely end in the death of the sick person.

Further Reading

Books:

Fairview Press. *Kids Write Through It*. Minneapolis, MN: Fairview Press, 1999.

Fitzgerald, Helen. *The Grieving Teen*. New York: Simon & Schuster, 2000

Gravelle, Kareen and John, Bertram A. *Teenagers Face-to-Face with Cancer*. New York: Messner, 1987.

Grollman, Earl A. *Straight Talk about Death for Teenagers: How to Cope with Losing Someone You Love*. Boston: Beacon Press, 1993.

Krementz, Jill. *How It Feels When a Parent Dies*. New York: Knopf, 1988.

Kübler-Ross, Elisabeth. *On Death and Dying*. New York: Macmillan Publishing Co., 1969.

Web:

www.campgoodgrief.com

www.compassionatefriends.org

www.diseases-explained.com

www.griefnet.org

www.groww.org

www.health.gov/nhic/

www.teenshealth.org

Index

About the Author

Heather Lehr Wagner is a writer and editor. She is the author of several books for teens, including *Understanding and Coping with Divorce* and *Blending Adopted and Foster Children into the Family* in the Focus on Family Matters series.

About the Editor

Marvin Rosen is a licensed clinical psychologist who practices in Media, Pennsylvania. He received his doctorate degree from the University of Pennsylvania in 1961. Since 1963, he has worked with intellectually and emotionally challenged people at Elwyn, Inc. in Pennsylvania, with clinical, administrative, research, and training responsibilities. He also conducts a private practice of psychology. Dr. Rosen has taught psychology at the University of Pennsylvania, Bryn Mawr College, and West Chester University. He has written or edited seven book and numerous professional articles in the areas of psychology, rehabilitation, emotional disturbance, and mental retardation.